AF362066

*Join my newsletter and get
my ebook library for FREE!*

INGO BLUM

Where Is My Little Unicorn?

Wo ist mein kleines Einhorn ?

ENGLISH/GERMAN

4

Where is Lily, my little unicorn?

Is she running over a rainbow?

Do you see her?

Wo ist Lily, mein kleines Einhorn?

Läuft sie über einen Regenbogen?

Siehst du sie?

6

Is she walking through a flower meadow?

Yes. Look, she is enjoying it!

Läuft sie durch eine Blumenwiese?

Ja. Schau, sie genießt es!

8

Is she hiding behind a tree?

Look, you can see her face!

What else do you see?

Versteckt sie sich hinter einem Baum?

Schau, du kannst ihr Gesicht sehen!

Was siehst du noch?

10

Is she talking to a fairy?

What are they talking about?

Spricht sie mit
einer Fee?

Worüber sprechen
sie?

Is she sleeping on a cloud?

Where is Lily?

Schläft sie auf einer Wolke?

Wo ist Lily?

14

Is she carrying a brave knight?

No, that's a horse, not a unicorn!

Trägt sie einen tapferen Ritter?

Nein, das ist ein Pferd, kein Einhorn!

16

Is she helping a wizard?

No, that's a dragon.

There is no unicorn

around.

Hilft sie einem Zauberer?

Nein, das ist ein Drache.

Es ist kein Einhorn

in der Nähe.

Is she living in a castle with a princess?

Look carefully! Do you see Lily?

Lebt sie in einem Schloss mit einer Prinzessin?

Schau genau hin!

Siehst du Lily?

Look, there she is!

She is flying in a wonderful balloon.

Bye, bye Lily!

Schau, da ist sie!

Sie fliegt in einem wunderschönen Ballon.

Tschüss, Lily!

Color the Unicorn

Mal das Einhorn aus.

More Bilingual Reading and Coloring Fun

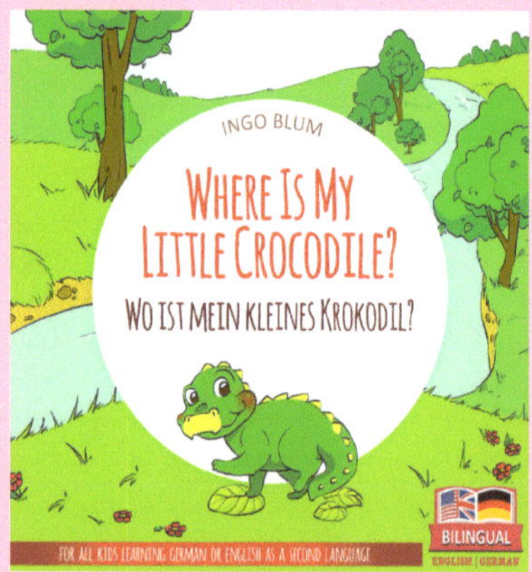

ISBN 978-1-982922-57-3

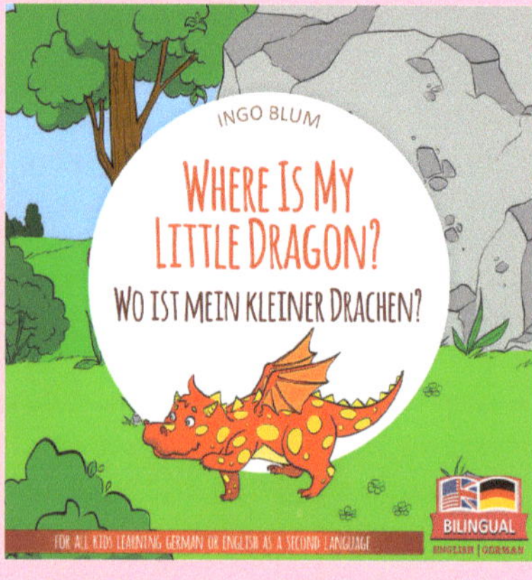

ISBN 978-1-982924-05-8

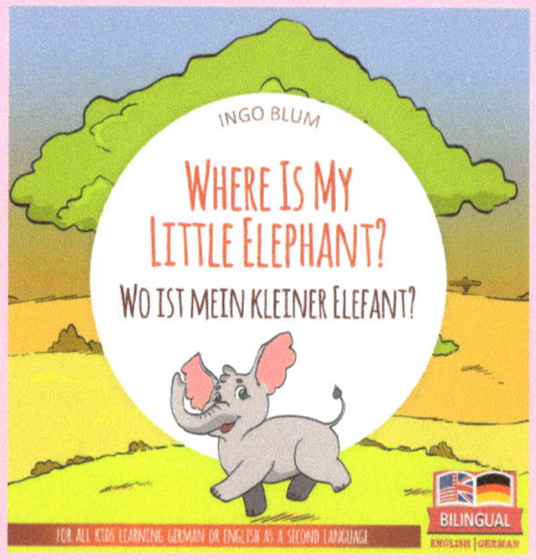

ISBN 978-1-982924-98-0

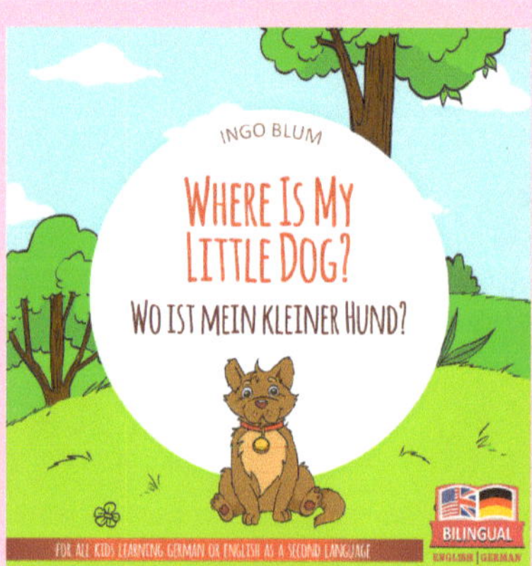

ISBN 978-1-982925-46-8

ISBN 979-8-672025-68-1

ISBN 979-8-682547-90-6

ISBN 978-1-983093-97-5

Scan the QR-code, get 5 ebooks for **FREE**!

bit.ly/5freebooks

Follow me on

 ingoblumauthor

 ingosplanet

 ingosplanet

www.ingramcontent.com/pod-product-compliance
Lightning Source LLC
LaVergne TN
LVHW071926160726
843515LV00010B/2535